In the interest of reaching every truth-seeking mind that desires to escape the path which leads to destruction of both body and soul, this tract is distributed free of charge as long as the issue lasts.

TRACT NO. 2

The Universal Publishing Association

P.O. Box 24027

Waco, Texas 76702

UniversalPublishing.com

ISBN: 978-1-962573-10-8

PRINTED IN U. S. A.

Introduction

The Need of Investigation

"God has precious light to come to His people. . . . When new light is presented to the church, it is perilous to shut yourself away from it. . . . To condemn that which you have not heard and do not understand will not exalt your wisdom in the eyes of those who are candid in their investigations of truth. And to speak with contempt of those whom God has sent with a message of truth is folly and madness. . . .

". . . for God will glorify His Word, that it may appear in a light in which we have *never before* beheld it. . . . Light will come to every earnest seeker for truth, *as* it came to Nathanael. . . . There should be liberty given for a frank investigation of truth, that *each* may know for himself what is the truth.

". . . if a message comes that you do not understand, take pains that you may hear the reasons the messenger may give, . . . for your position will not be shaken by coming in contact with error . . . . No one of those who imagine that they know it all is too old or too intelligent to learn from the humblest of the messengers of the living God."—*Testimonies On Sabbath School Work*, pp. 60-66.

As every important incident, in connection with the church, is preceded by a message, and as every such incident has been foretold by the prophets, it is important for each to realize

The Need of Prophecy.

Never in the annals of the Christian church has there been a shaking the like of that which is rapidly increasing as a result of the circulation of *The Shepherd's Rod* series of books and tracts throughout the rank and file of the Seventh-day Adventist denomination. It presents a singular and perplexing problem which human wisdom is utterly powerless to solve. In this extremity, then, we must turn to divine wisdom. Both the struggle and its remedy must be found in prophecy. Gladly, therefore, we accept the challenge: "Ask Me of things to come concerning My sons, and concerning the work of My hands command ye Me." Isa. 45:11.

Only when the church finds herself grounded on a reef of her own folly, with the fierce waves of divine retribution beating over her sides, is she in a position to realize her dreadful danger and her need of everything. And only when thus endangered and alarmed can she possibly be roused to the absolute necessity of having the gift of prophecy—her most imperative need in her present predicament. "Surely the Lord God will do nothing, but He revealeth *His secret* unto His servants the prophets." Amos 3:7. "Desire spiritual gifts, but rather that ye may *prophesy.* . . . He that prophesieth edifieth the church."

1 Cor. 14:1, 4. "For the testimony of Jesus is the *Spirit of Prophecy*." Rev. 19:10. Consequently, if she does not now awake to the fact that "where there is *no vision*, the people perish" (Prov. 29:18), then she never will.

Emphasizing the importance of the gifts of the Spirit, Paul says: "And he gave some, apostles; and some, *prophets*; and some, evangelists; and some, pastors and teachers; for the perfecting of the saints, for the work of the ministry, for the *edifying* of the *body* of Christ." Eph. 4:11, 12. "*After that* miracles, then gifts of healings, helps, governments, diversities of tongues." 1 Cor. 12:28.

But while most of these *gifts*, especially those of tongues and of governments, are zealously sought after by the churches, the one that was despised by the Jews—the gift of "*prophets*"—is wholly rejected by almost all Christendom. Therefore the spirit that instigated the killing of the ancient seers at the hand of the Jewish leaders, is today doing virtually the same sort of destructive work through organized religion.

The Jews, while ascribing praise and honor to the dead prophets who were slain by the forefathers, rejected the living prophets, thus bringing upon themselves the Master's mournful pronouncement:

"Woe unto you, scribes and Pharisees, hypocrites! because ye build the tombs of the prophets, and garnish the sepulchers of the righteous, and say, If we had been in the days of our fathers, we would not have been partakers with them in the blood of the prophets." Matt. 23:29, 30.

Present-day Christians who despise the gift of prophecy and deny to the gospel dispensation the authority of the Old Testament Scriptures, thereby reject all the prophets, though at the same time, they do them the lip service of acknowledging them as the servants of God. In giving such service, they are but building and garnishing the tombs of the prophets, as did the Jews, but when tested, they too, will be found to be liars. Mere lip professions of believing in the whole Bible, are worse than no profession at all, and doubly so when the professors are at the same time teaching that all the laws and statues, all the warnings and condemnations, apply only to the ancient Jews, whereas all the graces belong to the Christian church!

By following in this course, they have been led so far in perverting the gifts that their so-called gift of tongues is naught but gibberish, and is no more the Biblical gift than is Sunday the "sanctified" Sabbath day! Perverted also is the gift of governments, which is degenerated into an institution of prerogatives, formalities, goals, and the like, which, were they ever beneficial devices, are certainly, in their present low estate, nothing but agencies which in effect militate against the Truth, and neutralize the piety of the church. In this state of affairs, do the best of these professed Christians of today seem better than the worst of yesterday's Jews? Wherefore, O church of God, "Awake, Awake"! "Quench not the Spirit. *Despise not prophesyings.* Prove all things; hold fast that which is good." 1 Thess. 5:19-21. "Loose thyself from the [man-wrought] bands of thy neck, O captive daughter of Zion." Isa. 52:2.

As the gift of prophets is, according to the Scriptures, second in order of the gifts to the church, and the gift of governments and that of diversity of tongues are last, obviously, then, those who despise the gift of prophecy but exalt the gift of *governments* and the gift of *tongues*, are pulling the cart from its rear end, and are going in the wrong direction. To such, Christ is saying: "Knowest not that thou art wretched, and miserable, and poor, and blind, and naked." Rev. 3:17.

"Come now, and let us reason together, saith the Lord: though your sins be as scarlet, they shall be as white as snow; though they be red like crimson, they shall be as wool." Isa. 1:18.

This condition underlies the present church trouble, which along with its out-come is figuratively set forth in Zechariah's prophetic symbolism,

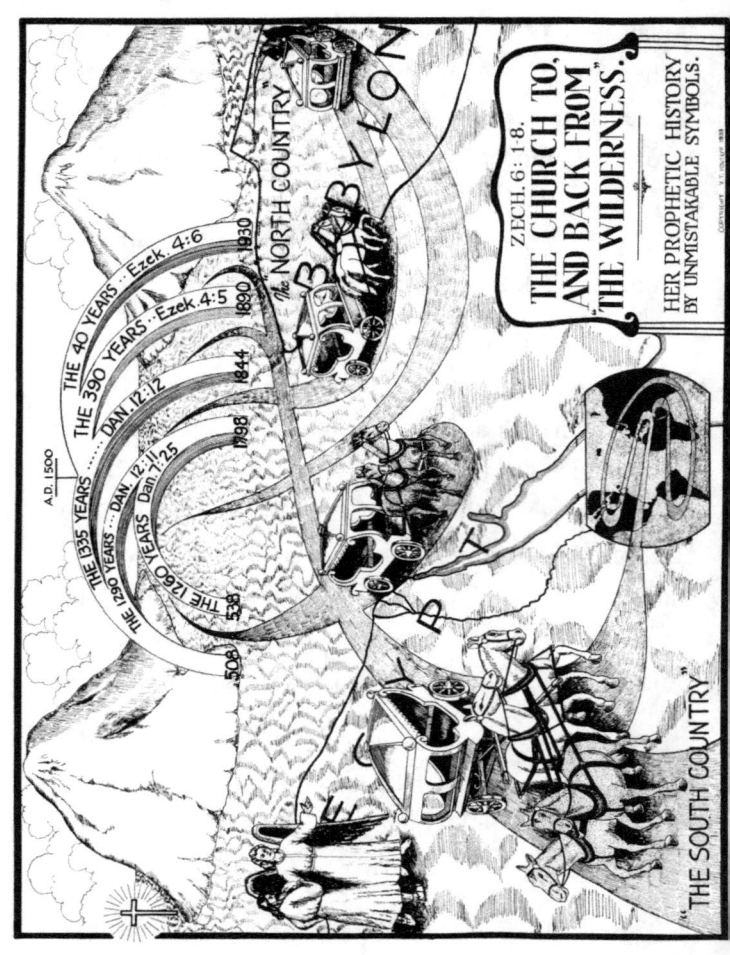

ZECH. 6: 1-8.

THE CHURCH TO, AND BACK FROM THE WILDERNESS.

HER PROPHETIC HISTORY BY UNMISTAKABLE SYMBOLS.

The NORTH COUNTRY

BABYLON

"THE SOUTH COUNTRY"

A.D. 1500

THE 40 YEARS ·· Ezek. 4:6

THE 390 YEARS ··· Ezek. 4:5

DAN. 12:12

THE 1335 YEARS

THE 1290 YEARS ··· DAN. 12:11

THE 1260 YEARS ··· Dan 7:25

1930

1690

1844

1798

538

508

The Paradox.

"And I turned, and lifted up mine eyes, and looked, and, behold, there came four chariots out from between two mountains; and the mountains were mountains of brass. In the first chariot were red horses; and in the second chariot black horses; and in the third chariot white horses; and in the fourth chariot grisled and bay horses. Then I answered and said unto the angel that talked with me, What are these, my lord? And the angel answered and said unto me, These are the four spirits of the heavens, which go forth from standing before the Lord of all the earth. The black horses which are therein go forth into the north country; and the white go forth after them; and the grisled go forth toward the south country. And the bay went forth, and sought to go that they might walk to and fro through the earth: and he said, Get you hence, walk to and fro through the earth. So they walked to and fro through the earth. Then cried he upon me, and spake unto me, saying, Behold, these that go toward the north country have quieted My spirit in the north country." Zech. 6:1-8.

These verses contain one of the most remarkable and important pictorial prophecies recorded in Sacred Writ, and their true interpretation brings a soul-gripping revelation of momentous church history. The first symbol to be considered is

Being composed of brass, the two mountains can never, in even the smallest part, be carried away by wind or flood. Matter not what betide them, they stand immovable. And as they are symbols of God's holy church (as seen from the scripture: "Thus saith the Lord; . . . *Jerusalem shall be called* a city of truth; and the mountain of the Lord of hosts the *holy mountain*"—Zech. 8:3), they must therefore represent her at a time when she is able to withstand the storm— when she is a clean and fit place for the dwelling of His Holy Presence which, as the mountains denote, is to His saints a mighty fortress and "an hiding place from the wind, and a covert from the tempest; as rivers of water in a dry place, as the shadow of a great rock in a weary land." Isa. 32:2. But "he that worketh deceit," says the Lord, "shall not dwell *within My house*: he that telleth lies shall not tarry in My sight." Ps. 101:7.

The facts so far established show God's Dwelling Place in two separate sections, for He has only one church organization at a time. The valley lying between the two mountains (the space through which the chariots come forth), therefore denotes the period between the two holy church organizations which the mountains represent.

This solid foundation promises a sure structure of truth which embraces church history culminating in a present-truth lesson of momentous consequence to everyone. Only if it reveals such a truth can we know that our interpretation is divinely inspired, not "private," and that it will stand every Bible test. In pursuance of this end, we now come to the consideration of

The Time of the Mountains'
Actual Existence.

When ancient Israel marched out of Egypt, "the Lord went before them by day in a pillar of a cloud, to lead them the way; and by night in a pillar of fire, to give them light; to go by day and night." "And in the place where the cloud abode, there the children of Israel pitched their tents." Ex. 13:21; Num. 9:17. But some years after the Israelitish movement had marched into the "promised land," God withdrew His personal presence from among them, because of their great sin of which they refused to repent.

"Therefore He brought upon them the king of the Chaldees, who . . . burnt the house of God, and brake down the wall of Jerusalem, and burnt all the palaces thereof with fire, and destroyed all the goodly vessels thereof. And them that had escaped from the sword carried he away to Babylon; where they were servants to him and his sons until the reign of the kingdom of Persia." 2 Chron. 36:17, 19, 20.

Were it not for the fact that a similar incident occurs in the Christian era, perhaps we would have to conclude without going further that the "two mountains" of "brass" are symbolical of the two sections of the church in Old Testament time. But inasmuch as the Dark Ages, from 538 A. D. to 1798 A. D. (Dan. 7:25; Rev. 12:6, 14), divide the Holy Mountain of God into two separate parts, we are compelled to prove from another angle the time to which these two figurative "mountains of brass" apply.

Never has this symbolical prophecy been understood by any people; and never *could it have been fulfilled and not been revealed* (for then would its truth have been *unavailable to the people in the past* and but half efficacious to us now). Necessarily, then, its fulfillment is yet future, sometime in the latter part of the Christian era.

The metal composing the "mountains" must represent that which is to make up what they stand for. Explicitly, the "*brass*" must disclose the people who are to make up two holy sections of the Christian church.

In the second chapter of Daniel, four empires are symbolized by a great metallic image of gold, silver, *brass*, and iron—a well understood prophecy of Babylon, Medo-Persia, Grecia, and Rome.

Gold, being first of value in the order of metals, is singularly adapted in symbolizing the *first* empire after the flood. Silver, being second to gold, is the number *two* metal, and exactly symbolizes the *second* empire—Medo-Persia. While brass, being third to gold, precisely fits the *third* empire (Grecia), and consequently has the numerical value of *three*.

So, being of brass, the "mountains" denote that the church which they symbolize is in period number three. And the fact that there is a third period, pre-supposes two preceding periods, making in all, three great divisions of time—the first, from creation to the flood; the second, from the flood to the crucifixion of Christ; and the third, from the crucifixion to His second coming. The *Christian era* is therefore the one to which the symbolical "mountains of brass" apply.

Necessarily, then, the former of the two "mountains" is symbolical of the spirit-filled early Christian church prior to 538 A. D., and the latter, of the Christian church sometime after 1798 A. D., when it is, as was the early Christian church, fitted for God's Holy Dwelling Place as described in the following scriptures: "O thou afflicted, tossed with tempest, and not comforted, behold, I . . . will make thy windows of agates, and thy gates of carbuncles . . . And *all* thy children shall be taught of the Lord; and great shall be the peace of thy children." Isa. 54:11-13.

This cannot be, as some may think, a symbolization of the Holy City, which comes "down from God out of heaven" (Rev. 21:2), for the celestial city has gates of "one pearl" (Rev. 21:21), whereas the gates which Isaiah describes are of "carbuncles." This symbolical language, therefore, can be descriptive only of the people who are to make up the spiritual house of God. (See Ephesians 2:20-22.) All her "stones" are of "fair colours": they are *all* precious jewels. No rubble, no "tares," no "lukewarm" professors are among her hosts, neither indeed can ever be, for, as is very easy to be seen, by the "foundations" are prefigured her founders; by the "windows," through which light shines, her living prophets or seers; and by the "gates of carbuncles" her "watchmen," who are to let in only those who have a right to enter, and to keep out all others. And the "borders of pleasant stones" are the members that beautify the house. Plainly, then, only "such as should be saved" will become a part of it.

"In righteousness shalt thou be *established*: thou shalt be far from oppression; for thou shalt *not fear*: and from terror; for it shall not come near thee. Behold, they *shall surely gather together*, but not by Me: whosoever shall gather together *against* thee shall *fall* for thy sake . . . and every tongue that shall rise against thee in judgment thou shalt condemn." Isa. 54:14, 15, 17.

This symbolically predicted church cannot be the Kingdom in the "New Earth," for then there shall be no wicked to gather against it, whereas against this church gather the wicked, whom she shall "condemn." And if she is to condemn them, then they are not condemned before they gather together against her.

"Clad in the armor of Christ's righteousness, the church is to enter upon her final conflict. 'Fair as the moon, clear as the sun, and terrible as an army with banners,' she is to go *forth into all the world*, conquering and to conquer."—*Prophets and Kings*, p. 725.

"Clad in complete armor of light and righteousness, she enters upon her final conflict. The dross, the worthless material, will be consumed, and the influence of the truth testifies to the world of its sanctifying, ennobling character."—*Testimonies to Ministers*, p. 17.

"Therefore thy gates shall be open continually; they shall not be shut day nor night; that men may bring unto thee the forces of the Gentiles, and that their kings may be brought. For the nation and kingdom that will not serve thee shall perish: yea, those nations shall be utterly wasted." Isa. 60:11, 12.

The church described in these passages is obviously not the church in her Laodicean state—"neither cold nor hot," and about to be spued out (Rev. 3:16). And since the symbolical mountains of brass are both alike, there being no distinction between them, therefore the second "mountain," the soon coming church of God, is to be of no less power and purity than that which characterized the first "mountain," the early Christian church, a glimpse of which is to be caught from the following scriptures:

"And when the day of Pentecost was fully come, they were *all* with *one accord* in one place. And they were *all filled with the Holy Ghost.* . . . and the *same day* there were added unto them about *three thousand* souls. And *the Lord added* to the church *daily such as should be saved.*" The Acts 2:1, 4, 41, 47.

"But a certain man named Ananias, with Sapphira his wife, sold a possession, and kept back part of the price. . . . But Peter said, Ananias, why hath Satan filled thine heart to lie to the Holy Ghost, and to keep back part of the price of the land? . . . And Ananias hearing these words fell down, and gave up the ghost. . . . And it was about the space of three hours after, when his wife, . . . came in. Then Peter said unto her, How is it that ye have agreed together to tempt the Spirit of the Lord? . . . Then fell she down straightway at his feet, and yielded up the ghost." The Acts 5:1-3, 5, 7, 9, 10.

Is there any comparison between the church described in The Acts and the one at the present time? Where is the power of the Holy Ghost in the church today? In the early church everyone was filled with It! Where do we read of the apostles' ever trying to raise financial goals? But how often do we hear that many of those who are brought into the church today, go out. And how few of those who remain are really converted to the Truth. Why such woeful waste, such pitiful loss? And why so many tares choking up the wheat? Jesus says: "*While men slept*, his enemy came and sowed tares among the wheat, and went his way." Matt. 13:25. Why?—obviously because the watchmen on the walls of Zion are asleep. (See *Testimonies*, Vol. 5, p. 235.)

Throwing light on this condition, the Spirit of Prophecy says: "What greater deception can come upon human minds than a confidence that they are right, when they are all wrong! *The message* of the True Witness *finds* the people of God in a sad deception, yet honest in that deception. . . . While those addressed are flattering themselves that they are in an exalted spiritual condition, the message of the True Witness breaks their security by the startling denunciation of their true condition of spiritual blindness, poverty, and wretchedness. The testimony, so cutting and severe, cannot be a mistake, for it is the True Witness who speaks, and his testimony must be correct."–*Testimonies*, Vol. 3, pp. 252, 253.

In trumpet tones, these all-too-evident facts declare that the church in her present condition, so unlike the early Christian church, cannot, therefore, be illustrated by the same symbol as was she. So, since the church today is as far from being like the early church as darkness is from light, the holy church of God symbolized by the second mountain of brass, must yet be in the future. Wherefore let us praise God that now within our reach is the glory of

The Church Triumphant!

When will the church really become God's Dwelling Place? By human effort it is as impossible to bring about such a change as it is to dry up the ocean. Only God can do it. But when He does, He will certainly make a clean work of it:

"And I will," He says, "fan them with a fan in the gates of the land; I will bereave them of children, I will destroy *My people*, since they return not from their ways." Jer. 15:7.

His "fan is in His hand, and He will thoroughly purge His floor, and gather His wheat into the garner; but He will burn up the chaff with unquenchable fire." Matt. 3:12.

"I saw that the Lord was whetting his sword in Heaven to cut them down. Oh that every lukewarm professor could realize the *clean* work that God is about to make among His professed people."—*Testimonies*, Vol. 1, p. 190.

"The Lord will work to purify His church. I tell you in truth, the Lord is about to turn and overturn in the institutions called by His name. Just how soon this refining process will begin, I can not say, but it will not be long deferred. He whose fan is in His hand will cleanse His temple of its moral defilement. He will thoroughly purge His floor."—*Testimonies to Ministers*, p. 373.

"The time has come for earnest and powerful efforts to rid the church of the slime and filth which is tarnishing her purity."—Id., p. 450.

Do not, my Brethren, say: "The vision that he seeth is for many days to come, and he prophesieth of the times that are far off." For "the days are at hand, and the effect of every vision." Ezek. 12:27, 23. "For Zion's sake will I not hold My peace," says the Lord, "and for Jerusalem's sake I will not rest, until the righteousness thereof go forth as brightness, and the salvation thereof as a lamp that burneth." Isa. 62:1.

"But the days of purification of the church are hastening on apace. God will have a people pure and true. In the mighty sifting soon to take place, we shall be better able to measure the strength of Israel. . . . Those who have trusted to intellect, genius, or talent, will not . . . stand at the head of rank and file" (*Testimonies*, Vol. 5, p. 80),

When The Church Is Fitly Represented By The Mountains.

Though the time of this solemn work—a subject of paramount importance to the church of God at this critical hour—is clearly set forth in the Bible and the Spirit of Prophecy, yet, ironically, it is a matter little thought of and little understood by the people in the church it concerns. We therefore at this point inquire further into it.

At the instance of Inspiration, the prophet Isaiah wrote: "For by fire and by His sword will the Lord plead with all flesh: and the slain of the Lord shall be many. . . . And I will send those that escape of them unto the nations, . . . and they shall bring all your brethren . . . in a clean vessel into the house of the Lord." Isa. 66:16, 19, 20.

Note that these prophetic words say that those who "*escape*" being among "the slain of the Lord" are to be sent "unto the nations," and that they "shall declare [His] glory among the Gentiles. And . . . shall bring *all* [their] brethren . . . *out of all nations*."

As this great world-wide work of ingathering cannot be done after probation has closed, you must not let the enemy deceive you "with good words and fair speeches." Show him that he cannot explain these inspired passages another way, and yet have his explanation in harmony with what the Lord has said in the foregoing scripture as well as in the following statement from the Spirit of Prophecy:

"While the investigative judgment is going forward in heaven . . . there is to be a special work of purification . . . among God's people upon earth. . . . Then the church which our Lord at His coming is to receive to Himself will be 'a glorious church, not having spot, or wrinkle, or any such thing.' Then she will look forth 'as the morning, fair as the moon, clear as the sun, and terrible as an army with banners.' "—*The Great Controversy*, p. 425.

This statement from the Spirit of Prophecy also clearly indicates that the purification takes place before probation closes, or "while the investigative judgment is going forward in heaven," and that then the church, clean and spotless, is to go into all the world conquering and to conquer (*Prophets and Kings*, p. 725).

Brother, Sister, do not rise up against this message of deliverance, and by so doing join the ranks of the enemy, who sowed the tares in the church, and who is determined to keep them there, for he knows that with a purified church, his power will be crushed, and the barriers which he has erected against it will be smashed to fragments! Indeed, "we need never expect that when the Lord has light for His people, Satan will stand calmly by and make no effort to prevent them from receiving it. He will work upon minds to excite distrust and jealousy and unbelief."—*Testimonies*, Vol. 5, p. 728.

From the evidences adduced, the fact towers forth that the purification takes place before the work of the gospel is finished in any part of the world: for those who "*escape*" the slaughter are sent to "bring all [their] brethren for an offering unto the Lord *out of* all nations." Necessarily therefore, the consummation of this "special work of purification" precedes the commencement of "The Loud Cry." Doubly conclusive proof of this is that the Spirit of Prophecy states that "the true people of God, who have the spirit of the work of the Lord, . . . will always be on the side of faithful and plain dealing with sins. . . . Especially in the closing work for the church, in the sealing time of the one hundred and forty-four thousand. . . ." This special work of purification and "sealing of the servants of God is the same that was shown to Ezekiel in vision."—*Testimonies*, Vol. 3, p. 266: *Testimonies to Ministers*, p. 445.

Ezekiel's vision discloses that those who "sigh and cry for all the abominations that be done in the midst thereof" (the church) are marked, or sealed, and that the men with the "slaughter weapons" then "slay utterly old and young, both maids, and little children, and women" who have not the mark. The purification of the church, therefore, is a separation of the sinners from the true people of God. At the time of its fulfillment, the immediate future, the 144,000 receive the seal, or mark, escape the slaughter, become the "servants of God," and go forth unto the nations to finish the work. This makes them the "first-fruits" of the living who are to be translated, and "all their brethren" whom they bring in (the "great multitude" of Revelation 7, verse 9), the second fruits of the living who are to be translated: for where there are no second fruits, there can be no first. (For further light on this subject, read Tract No. 1, *Pre-"Eleventh Hour" Extra!*.)

Brethren, we must "sigh and cry" against the sins in the church; not against the message which is to seal us for translation and make us a people fitly symbolized by the mountain of brass. Your sighing and crying for the abominations done in her "midst," makes you eligible for the "mark"; but should you attempt to shield the abominations, you shall fall under the slaughter weapons of the angels. The church is to be purified and made clean and fit to be God's Dwelling Place. In no other way can she be identified as the "mountain of brass," the symbol of endurance. This is the church that shall 'enter upon her final conflict," and the one with whom the dragon is to be "wroth:" for the symbolical "woman" and "her seed," *as a body, keep* the commandments of God and have the "testimony of Jesus Christ." Rev. 12:17.

Having fully cleared the first part of Zechariah's symbolism, we now give attention to

The Valley Between The Mountains.

The truth having been solidly established that the early Christian church is symbolized by one of the "brass mountains," and the church that closes the gospel work, by the other, then it follows as a logical sequence that the valley between, from which come the four chariots, must be symbolical of the period from the one church to the other. The next symbolism, then, to be considered is

The Four Chariots.

Says the prophet Zechariah: "In that day shall there be upon the *bells of the horses*, HOLINESS UNTO THE LORD." Zech. 14:20. As symbols to illustrate various lessons, horses are quite prominently employed in the Scriptures, being in every instance perfectly adapted, of course, to the circumstance or situation. In this connection, they represent people, for the sounding of their "bells" is "HOLINESS

UNTO THE LORD"; whereas "the spasmodic, fitful movements of some who claim to be Christians is well represented by the work of strong but untrained *horses*. When one pulls forward, another pulls back." — *Testimonies to Ministers*, pp. 489, 490.

These symbolical "horses," therefore, each portray a certain class of people in connection with the church. And owing to the fact that each team is leading a chariot, they can denote only a class of church leaders. The chariots, consequently, must in some way depict the church membership which the symbolical horses are leading. Moreover, to Zechariah's question, "What are these, my lord? . . . the angel answered and said, . . . These are the four spirits of the *heavens*, which go forth *from standing before* the Lord of all the earth." Zech. 6:4, 5. Hence these symbolisms stand for heaven-born messages carried by the church on earth. And since the symbolism is self-defining, it answers the question:

Why Chariot Symbol of a Church?

The Scriptures symbolize God's church by various earthly objects. To illustrate: "In that day," says the Lord, "will I make Jerusalem a burdensome *stone* for all people: all that burden themselves with it shall be cut in pieces." Zech. 12:3. "Thou shalt also be a *crown* of glory in the hand of the Lord." Isa. 62:3. "And the seven *candlesticks* which thou sawest are the seven churches." Rev. 1:20.

The same object cannot perfectly characterize the church under varying conditions and circumstances or relationships. For example, on the one hand the church that gave birth to Christ (Rev. 12:1, 2) cannot congruously be symbolized by a chariot, but rather only by a woman, while on the other hand the church with which God will break the nations, cannot congruously be likened to a woman, but rather to a "stone" (Dan. 2:45), or an "axe." Jer. 51:20. For a church in its work of gathering souls, the most fitting symbol is a "chariot," and for its leadership, naturally "horses."

As there are, in the symbolization before us, four chariots to be identified, we must therefore consider each one separately, beginning with

The First Chariot.

The consecutive order of the chariots indicates a series of gospel events. "In the first chariot were red horses." That the color red stands for bloodshed, the Spirit of Prophecy bears out: "As we were traveling along, we met a company. . . . I noticed *red* as a border on their garments. . . . I asked Jesus who they were. He said they were *martyrs* that had been slain for Him."—*Early Writings*, pp. 18,19. The red border on the garments of this company being emblematic of martyrdom, obviously, then, the red color of the "horses" denotes the martyred leaders of the church before 538 A. D.

In response to Zechariah's question as to who the horses were and where they were going, the angel answered: "The black horses which are therein go forth into the north country; and the white go forth after them; and the grisled go forth toward the south country. And the bay went forth, and sought to go that they might walk to and fro through the earth." Zech. 6:6, 7. Though the angel's answer discloses the respective directions toward which the black, white, grisled, and bay horses went, it omits to make the slightest mention of the red horses, thus riveting the conclusion that the red horses were martyred and went nowhere so far as their final destination is concerned. This being clear, our next step, logically, is to identify

The Second Chariot.

"And in the second chariot [were] black horses." Universally, the figurative significance of "black" is bondage. So as the martyrdom of the early Christian church was followed by the Dark Ages of religion, from 538 A. D. to 1798 A. D., it is very evident that the chariot with the black horses represents the church and its leadership during this long prophetic period in Ecclesiastical Roman bondage. This fact is borne out by the angel's explanation of the horses' destination: "The black horses," he said, ". . . go forth into the north country." And "the north country" is the Biblical term for ancient Babylon, as is quickly seen from the following scriptures:

". . . saith the Lord God; . . . I will bring . . . Nebuchadnezzar king of *Babylon*, . . . from the *north*." Ezek. 26:7. Again: when the Jews were returning from Babylon to Jerusalem, God spoke through His prophet Zechariah, saying: "Ho, ho, come forth, and flee from *the land of the north*" (Zech. 2:6), thus identifying Babylon as "the north country." But as we are dealing with the fulfillment of prophecy in the New Testament era, the north country in this connection must be antitypical Babylon—Christianized Rome— where God's people during the New Testament period have gone. This clear-cut truth concerning the second chariot, leads us to the exposition of

The Third Chariot.

And there were "in the third chariot white horses." Since black is significant of bondage, then white, being the opposite of black, must denote liberty. Accordingly, the white horses with their chariot must be symbolical of the church, following her 1260 year period of Roman bondage. Said the angel to Zechariah: "The *white* go forth after" the black horses, to the *north country*. The white chariot therefore represents a free church, carrying a heaven-born message to the north country shortly after 1798 A. D., in time of *liberty*. The only such message found on record is that of the Millerite movement, of which we read:

"To William Miller and his co-laborers it was given to preach the warning in America. This country became the *center* of the great Advent Movement. . . . The writings of Miller and his associates were carried to *distant lands*. *Wherever missionaries had penetrated in all the world*, were sent the glad tidings of Christ's speedy return."—*The Great Controversy*, p. 368.

But though "white horses" went to the "north country," the Millerites, or "First Advent Movement," was not in response to the call, "come out of her My people." This is made clear by Miller's own words: "In all my labors . . . I never had the desire or thought to establish any separate interest from that of existing denominations, or to benefit one at the expense of another. I thought to benefit all."—*The Great Controversy*, p. 375.

The concluding revelation is: "Behold, these that go toward the *north country* have *quieted My Spirit in the north country*." Zech. 6:8. After the warning message by the Millerite movement had been rejected by the churches, in fulfillment of the words, "*have quieted My Spirit in the north country*," God withdrew His Spirit from them. In evidence of this, "the Second Angel" announced: "Babylon is fallen." Rev. 14:8.

The foregoing chain of facts surrounding the first three symbolical "chariots," shows that the series of gospel events which they comprehend terminated with the Millerite movement in 1844 A. D. And the additional fact that the 'white' color of the "horses" also denotes purity, shows that the "third chariot" is symbolical of the church which of all the seven churches is the only one that is white, without condemnation—the Philadelphian church (Rev. 3:7).

The Word of God is full of meaning; its depth unfathomable; and its truth, like the waves that ever break on the shore-line, leaving the shore of life with never-ceasing waves, one of which brings in the fact that the Millerite church's being named "Philadelphia" was not merely incidental. The name, meaning "brotherly love," was divinely designed, and will not, in all the Christian era, fit a church organization other than the Millerite—the only one that is not guilty of casting out its brethren for hearing a message from God, or of restricting their religious freedom in investigating for themselves any purported truths! It alone, therefore, stands free from the guilt and condemnation underlined in the Lord's charge:

"Hear the word of the Lord, ye that tremble at His word; *Your brethren that hated you, that cast you out for My name's sake*, said, Let the Lord be glorified: but He shall appear to your joy, and *they shall be ashamed*." Isa. 66:5. These heaven-condemned, because self-appointed, judges entered not in themselves, and them that were entering in, they hindered (Luke 11:52). To repeat: the Millerite, or "First Advent Movement," being the only one that never cast out any of its brethren, is consequently the only church which can be represented by the white chariot, and the only one worthy of the name "Philadelphia"—"brotherly love."

All seven of these antitypical churches (Rev. 2 and 3) started out well, but sooner or later Satan succeeded in bringing into each one in succession a flood of satanic agencies (figuratively, the "tares") in the garb of professed believers of the Truth. Especially has this been so with the ministry, by whom he has been able to lead entire churches astray. And always some of the members who have refused to follow the leadership of man in the place of that of Christ, have been cast out. Indeed, whenever God has sent a message to His church, the ministry, instead of standing by the messenger and helping get the message to the people, has fought against it, standing, almost as a unit, in its way, so that it not reach the people! Showing how the ministry tried to put an extinguisher on the

"First Advent Message," and how they persecuted the laity who dared attend Miller's preaching, church history says:

"But as ministers and religious leaders decided against the advent doctrine, and desired to suppress all agitation of the subject, they not only opposed it from the pulpit, but denied their members the privilege of attending preaching upon the second advent, or even of speaking of their hope in the social meetings of the church." ". . . therefore it was largely committed to humble laymen. Farmers left their fields, mechanics their tools, traders their merchandise, professional men their positions; and yet the number of workers was small in comparison with the work to be accomplished."—*The Great Controversy*, pp. 376, 368.

"The work did not stand in the wisdom and learning of men, but in the power of God. It was not the most talented, but the most humble and devoted, who were the first to hear and obey the call. . . . Those who had formerly led in the cause were among the last to join in this movement."—Id., p. 402. "The fact that the message was, to a great extent, preached by laymen, was urged as an argument against it. As of old, the plain testimony of God's Word was met with the inquiry, 'Have any of the rulers or of the Pharisees believed?' . . . Multitudes, trusting implicitly to their pastors, refused to listen to the warning;

and others, though convinced of the truth, dared not confess it, lest they should be 'put out of the synagogue.'" —Id., p. 380.

". . . The true followers of Christ . . . do not wait for truth to become popular. Being convinced of their duty, they deliberately accept the cross."—Id., p. 460. "The half-hearted and superficial could no longer lean upon the faith of their brethren."—Id., p. 395. "Instead of questioning and caviling concerning that which they do not understand, let them give heed to the light which already shines upon them, and they will receive greater light."—Id., p. 528.

"There has ever been a class professing godliness, who, instead of following on to know the truth, make it their religion to seek some fault of character or error of faith in those with whom they do not agree. Such are Satan's right-hand helpers."—Id., p. 519.

"All who look for hooks to hang their doubts upon, will find them. And those who refuse to accept and obey God's word until every objection has been removed, and there is no longer an opportunity for doubt, will never come to the light."—Id., p. 527.

Of all "the seven churches" (Rev. 2 and 3), only the Philadelphian (the Millerite) church did not run afoul these same satanic practices. Ever true to God, it closed its brief but spotless career in 1844, its appointed destination. Having lived its entire life under the personal supervision of its founder, it was never new-modeled. Thus being without condemnation, as perfectly illustrated by the third "chariot" and its "white horses," it stands out in bold relief to the succeeding movement, represented by

The Fourth Chariot.

Since the first three "chariots" embrace the history of the church up to 1844 A. D., the fourth one must represent a subsequent church organization—successor to the Millerite, or Philadelphian church. The last of "the seven churches," the church of the "Laodiceans," necessarily, therefore, is the one symbolized by the fourth "chariot."

Amidst the multi-sectarian confusion overspreading all Christendom at the present time, it may seem difficult to segregate the Laodiceans from among the rest. But the great Designer of types and symbols, the One Who seeing the end from the beginning, thus foresaw precisely what was to be the condition and the work of the last of "the seven churches," must therefore by His Word, be able to pick this church from among the multitude of churches, and set it like a beacon, shining forth in the darkest hour of the night.

But even as Satan put forth determined efforts to misapply the name "Philadelphia," and thus to obscure it from view and cause it to go unnoticed, so has he confused

The Name of the Last Chariot.

Just as the name "Philadelphia" fits only one church organization, and only one of the chariots, so the name "Laodiceans" can logically fit only one of the chariots and only one denomination. The word, itself, is derived from the Greek word, *Lego-dikean*, meaning, "declaring judgment." After the event of the Philadelphian church, there must therefore be a church declaring judgment. And it is a historical fact that in 1844 A. D., the very year the Millerite movement came to the end of its appointed course, a new movement, the Seventh-day Adventist denomination, arose, proclaiming: "Fear God, and give glory to Him; for the hour of *His judgment is come*." Rev. 14:7.

In spite of the unenviable record of the Laodicean church, the founder of its movement, unlike the founders of other movements, honestly states in *Testimonies*, Vol. 3, p. 252: "The message to the church of the Laodiceans is a startling denunciation, and is applicable to the people of God at the present time"— the Seventh-day Adventists. Declaring the judgment, as well as being in the undone condition described, the S.D.A. church is the only one which can rightly be called the "Laodicean,"—Declaring Judgment. What an absolute match between description and condition!

"O magnify the Lord with me, and let us exalt His name together," for He hath "magnified [His] Word above all [His] name." Ps. 34:3; 138:2.

Since both the third chariot and the Philadelphian church have been identified as representing the Millerite movement, and also since the Laodicean church has been identified as representing the Seventh-day Adventist movement, then it incontrovertibly follows that the "fourth chariot," the last of the chariots, is symbolical of the S. D. A. church—the Laodicean.

Now if this application of "the chariot" is wrong, the simple and positive proof is, of course, that it cannot be made congruously to fit the S. D. A. church, but if it is right, then, by the same token, it cannot be made congruously to fit any other but the Adventist church: for the divine symbols are devised perfectly to fit only one object. The final test, therefore, of the interpretation herein given, is the conclusiveness of the paradoxical part of the symbolism—

The Grisled and The Bay—Double Leadership.

And in the "fourth chariot" were "*grisled* and *bay* horses." The anomalous part of this symbolical prophecy is, manifestly, that the fourth chariot, unlike the other three, has a double span of horses. But most arresting about the whole symbolism is the paradoxical fact that the *grisled went "toward the south country*, and the bay went forth, and . . . *walked to and fro through the earth"!* Zech. 6:6, 7. The grisled go one way, and the bay, another way, and yet both are pulling the same chariot!

Obviously, therefore, this strange circumstance must hold a singular present truth lesson of great importance to the church of God at the present hour, when the vision has been opened and the truth unfolded, the time in which the church is confronted with a strange and perplexing problem which human wisdom is at a loss to solve.

The dissimilar teams hitched to the fourth chariot, each pulling in a different direction from the other, show not only that there is a double leadership in the Laodicean church, but also that the one is opposed to the other in character as well as in purpose. This condition being a strange one, the wise will well consider it. Seeing that the Word of God has spoken it, and that the symbolism perfectly describes the contest which, before their very eyes, is taking place, they will tenaciously take hold of the truth.

Now for the explanation of the climactic and enigmatic part of this symbolization, we must go to the past and present record of the Laodicean church. As the message to every church is addressed to the "angel" who has charge of the candlestick (the church—Rev. 1:20), John was instructed: "And *unto the angel* of the church of the Laodiceans write." Rev. 3:14. But this "angel" cannot be a heavenly angel, for he is at fault: "Neither cold nor hot," but "wretched, and miserable, and poor, and blind, and naked" "*and knowest not*." Rev. 3:16, 17. What else could this angel be but the earthly one who is given charge over the "candlestick"? Plainly, therefore, he and the servant "whom his Lord hath made *ruler over His household*, to give them meat in due season" (Matt. 24:45) are identical, both of whom, clearly, represent the church leadership, not the membership.

Anyone having a reasonable knowledge of the Scriptures, should know that God cannot finish His work on earth with a "wretched, and miserable, and poor, and blind, and naked" leadership; and what is worse, one that does not even know its condition. Those who are excusing the overwhelming wickedness everywhere, are not God's true people; they are the 'tares,' the seed of the Evil One.

"The message God sends through His servants," says the Spirit of Prophecy, "will be scorned and derided by *unfaithful shepherds*, who tread down with their feet the feed of the pastures, giving the flock as food that which they have defiled. 'Woe be unto the Pastors that destroy and scatter the sheep of My pasture! saith the Lord.' "—*Review and Herald*, June 25, 1901.

In view of this sad fact, God must have a second leadership to finish His greatest work since the world began. Of this second set of servants, we read: "And I saw another angel ascending from the east, having the seal of the living God: and he cried with a loud voice to the four angels, . . . saying, Hurt not the earth, neither the sea, nor the trees, till we have sealed *the servants* of our God in their foreheads." "And in their mouth was found *no guile*: for they are *without fault* before the throne of God." Rev. 7:2, 3; 14:5.

Thus by testimony and by symbol, the Word of God brings to view two dissimilar classes of "servants"— the one "*lukewarm*," the other "*without fault*."

So important is this subject that the Spirit of Prophecy turns the light on still another aspect of it:

"But the days of *purification* of the church are hastening on apace. God will have a people pure and true. . . . Those who have trusted to intellect, genius, or talent, will not then stand at the head of rank and file."—*Testimonies*, Vol. 5, p. 80.

The fact that our conferences grant ministerial licenses only to college graduates, shows that they are trusting to human wisdom

—wisdom which God can no more use now than He could when Moses displayed it. And the fact that they have been following in this foolish course for years, is another unimpeachable evidence in the proof that the ministry at the present time is comprised of men whom God cannot use, not only because they are independent of Him, but also because against His will they have kept out of the work those whom He can use:

"Now I want to say, God has not put any kingly power in our ranks to control this or that branch of the work. The work has been greatly restricted by the efforts to control it in every line. Here is a vineyard presenting its barren places that have received no labor. And if one should start out to till these places in the name of the Lord, unless he should get the permission of the men in a little circle of authority, he would receive no help. God means that His workers shall have help. If a hundred should start out on a mission to destitute fields, crying unto God, He would open the way before them.

"Let me tell you, if your heart is in the work, and you have faith in God, you need not depend upon the sanction of any minister or any people: if you go right to work in the name of the Lord, in a humble way doing what you can to teach the truth, God will vindicate you.

"If the work had not been so restricted

by an impediment here, and an impediment there, and on the other side an impediment, it would have gone forward in its majesty. It would have gone in weakness at first; but the God of heaven lives."—*Review and Herald*, April 16, 1901.

Not until Paul had forsaken all trust in human wisdom, counting it loss for Christ, was God able to exalt him in His mighty hand. "And I brethren," says the great apostle, ". . . *came not* with excellency of speech or of wisdom, declaring unto you the testimony of God." 1 Cor. 2:1. But unlike the humbled Paul, the great men in the church today "are self-sufficient, independent of God, and he cannot use them . . . The call to *this* great and solemn work *was*," since 1844, "presented to men of learning and position; had these been little in their own eyes, and trusted fully in the Lord, He would have honored them with bearing His standard in triumph to the victory. But they separated from God, yielded to the influence of the world, and the Lord *rejected* them."—*Testimonies*, Vol. 5, pp. 80, 82.

But "the Lord has faithful servants, who *in the shaking*, testing time will be *disclosed to view*. There are precious ones *now hidden* who have not bowed the knee to Baal. They *have not* had the light which has been shining in a concentrated blaze *upon you*. But it may be under a *rough and uninviting exterior* the pure brightness of a genuine *Christian character* will be revealed."—*Testimonies*, Vol. 5, pp. 80, 81.

Thus in their perfect mutual harmony, the Bible and the Spirit of Prophecy once again exalt each other, and clear the paradox of the fourth chariot—its double span of horses each of which, as revealed by their colors and aims, is inimical in character, principle, and objective; each contesting the right to the chariot. Endeavoring to keep it in the south country (Egypt), where they are blindly "settled on their lees," the grisled, the leadership at the very head of the chariot, "say in their heart, The Lord will not do good, neither will He do evil. Therefore their *goods* shall become a booty, and their houses a desolation." Zeph. 1:12, 13. Whereas the bay, the leadership behind the grisled, seek to go to and fro through the earth.

The former say: "He is too merciful to visit His people in judgment" by fulfilling Ezekiel 9 upon them, while the latter sigh and cry for the abominations in the midst thereof. Thus whereas behind the grisled horses there is a crying of God's visitation, there is ahead of the bay, a crying of "peace and safety . . . from men who will *never again* lift up their voice like a trumpet to show *God's people* their transgressions and the house of Jacob their sins. These dumb dogs, that would not bark," says the founder of the church, "are the ones who feel the just vengeance of an offended God. Men, maidens, and little children, all perish together." —*Testimonies*, Vol. 5, p. 211.

While on the one hand, therefore, we prophetically behold the failure of the grisled horses to maintain control of the chariot (church) because of their dereliction of duty, on the other hand we see the bay horses both prophetically and actually getting ready to take over the chariot at the appointed time; or, as the angel, speaking in prophetic past, explained: they "sought to go that they might walk to and fro through the earth." Zech. 6:7.

Unlike in color, the two teams are figurative of two classes of servants unlike in character. The former class (the grisled) are "men of learning and position," but "self-sufficient, independent of God, and He cannot use them." The latter (the bay), those whom "He will raise up and exalt among us," are "those who are taught rather by the unction of his Spirit, than by the outward training of scientific institutions. . . . God will manifest that he is not dependent on learned, self-important mortals."—*Testimonies*, Vol. 5, p. 82.

This latter class, moreover, have the "pure brightness of a genuine Christian character," "but, it may be under a *rough and uninviting exterior*"—unveneered by "higher education" so-called. "He will use men for the accomplishment of His purpose

—43—

whom some of the brethren would reject as unfit to engage in the work."—*Review and Herald*, Feb. 9, 1885. "And I will gather the remnant of My flock out of all countries whither I have driven them, and will bring them again to their folds; and they shall be fruitful and *increase*. And I will set up shepherds over them which shall *feed them*: and they shall fear no more, nor be dismayed, neither shall they be lacking, saith the Lord." Jer. 23:3, 4.

Though these servants of God, who are to be disclosed to view during the *purification* of the church, "have not had the light which has been shining in a concentrated blaze" upon the others, yet it is stated of them: "The most weak and hesitating in the church, will be as David—willing to do and dare. . . . Then will the church of Christ appear 'fair as the moon, clear as the sun, and terrible as an army with banners.' " "She is to go forth into all the world, conquering and to conquer."—*Testimonies*, Vol. 5, pp. 81, 82; *Prophets and Kings*, p. 725.

Where else in all Christendom, save in the S. D. A. Denomination (the church of the Laodiceans), is to be found the fulfilment of the prophetic church history unfolded in this study? If this startling revelation of present truth, plain and certain as the conflict itself between Good and Evil, does not reach the Laodicean heart, then nothing can ever reach it. O, Brother, Sister, be not fooled: if this does not reach your heart now in time to save you from the evil to come, it will surely overtake you eventually, but then only to destroy, not to save, you. So stay no longer with the grisled horses in Egypt, for to do so will be only to perish there with them while

The Bay Take The Chariot To
The Promised Land.

Seeing that the chariot is drawn by both teams each pulling in a different direction from the other, obviously both cannot win out without breaking it in two, thus leaving it ruined and useless. One pair or the other, therefore, must be cut out of the traces. And the fact that the bay (the strong horses"—verse 3, margin) are the ones who "walk to and fro through the earth" while the grisled remain in Egypt, shows that the bay alone are to possess the chariot and to take it from Egypt to the promised land.

Although this remarkable prophetic symbolization, now opened up fully, was simply another locked prophecy when *The Shepherd's Rod*, Vol.1 was published and sent throughout the S. D. A. denomination in 1930, yet in its momentous message to Laodicea (declaring that the prophecy of the ninth chapter of Ezekiel is on the verge of fulfillment, and that those who escape the "slaughter" will comprise the future leadership of the church), the warning-tragedy in the singular paradox here revealed, was anticipated. Thus we see that from the very first, *The Shepherd's Rod*, in projecting a preview of the same critical problem encountered in the warning-paradox here revealed, was published in pre-clarification of Zechariah's prophecy! And, reciprocally, not only does this remarkable prediction make the Word of God appear more marvelous than ever before, but also it sustains the message in *The Shepherd's Rod*, and unveils the outcome of the baffling difficulty before us, the like of which has never occurred in the history of the church.

Though the leaders of the S. D. A. denomination are determined to drive out of the church all who believe in the message of *The Shepherd's Rod*, they are trying to make it appear that the *Rod's* adherents are pulling out for themselves. The paradoxical truth, however, shows that they are to possess "the chariot," and their refusing to leave the church demonstrates in actuality the certainty of the bay horses' alone taking the chariot to its destination—"to and fro through the earth."

The revelation of this warning-paradox also demonstrates that God controls the Scriptures and brings them to light at just the very time His people need to know which way to turn! And now, having found the way, let us, as did the apostles, tarry in the church with the message until told,

"Get you hence, walk to and fro through the earth." Having thus done our part, it will be said of us: "Kings of armies did flee apace: and *she that tarried at home* (church) divided the spoil. Though ye have lien among the pots, yet shall ye be as the wings of a dove covered with silver, and her feathers with yellow gold." Ps. 68:12, 13.

So whereas the bay horses are now getting themselves groomed to go "to and fro through the earth," the grisled are endeavoring to kick the bay away from the chariot and to keep it in

The South Country.

To determine the antitypical significance of the "south country," we consult the Revelation: "And I will give power unto My two Witnesses, and They shall prophesy a thousand two hundred and threescore days, clothed in sackcloth. And when They shall have finished Their testimony, the beast that ascendeth out of the bottomless pit shall make war against Them, and shall overcome Them, and kill Them. And Their dead bodies shall lie in the street of the great city, which spiritually is called Sodom and Egypt, where also our Lord was crucified." Rev. 11:3, 7, 8.

"The two Witnesses," says the Spirit of Prophecy, "represent the Scriptures of the Old and the New Testament. . . . They continued their testimony throughout the entire period of 1260 years. . . . The period when the two Witnesses were to prophesy clothed in sackcloth, ended in 1798. . . . It was in 1793 that the decrees which abolished the Christian religion and set aside the Bible [or killed the 'two Witnesses'], passed the French Assembly."—*The Great Controversy*, pp. 267, 268, 287.

Since, therefore, the atheistic French government in 1793 is called by the Scriptures "Sodom and Egypt, where also our Lord was crucified," ancient Egypt—"the south country"—is symbolical of our present world *in general*, where "our Lord was crucified." Consequently, though "the black" and "the white horses" went "into the north country" (Christendom), "the grisled horses" went toward "the south country" (the world).

In remarkable corroboration of this particular phase of the prophecy, the Seventh-day Adventist denomination, after the disappointment in 1844, went forth in fulfilment of the following divine commission: "Thou must prophesy again before many peoples, and nations, and tongues, and kings." Rev. 10:11. Thus does "the more sure word of prophecy," borne out in detail by church history, establish the fact that the message of the S. D. A. denomination has gone to the world—Egypt. Hence, the danger of the "fourth chariot" (the S. D. A.'s) is not of going into Babylon, but rather into Egypt.

In further confirmation of this plain and alarming prophetic fact, the Spirit of Prophecy says: "I am filled with sadness when I think of our condition as a people. . . . The church has *turned back* from following Christ her Leader, and is steadily *retreating toward Egypt*. Yet *few* are alarmed or astonished at their want of spiritual power."—*Testimonies*, Vol. 5, p. 217.

But some with the fabled ostrich-habit of burying the head to danger shout up from under the sand, as it were, "there is no danger. This movement will triumph." But the very best evidence that the great objective of the S. D. A. movement is in the gravest danger of failing, is the deep concern evinced by the president of the General Conference, in an address published in the *Review and Herald*, Oct. 14, 1937, which we quote in part as follows:

"I tell you solemnly that there are forces and influences at work which, if unchecked, will render us just as unprepared for the *second* coming of Christ as was Israel for His *first* coming. Make no mistake about that. I see those influences at work. The spirit of Sadduceeism is working like leaven, and I want to lift my voice in earnest entreaty that you may see that the door is closed against all such intrusions. . . . I summon you all to engage in the fight against the spirit of Sadduceeism, the spirit of worldly conformity, the spirit which, if allowed to go unchecked, will subvert and change the whole spirit and purpose of this movement. . . . This question also came to me: Are we, in our defense of these great principles of truth that God has committed to us, allowing the mantle to fall from our own shoulders upon the shoulders of others? Are we going to allow others to step into our places and call the world to a reformation along some of these lines?

"Objective of Movement in the Balance

"I believe that we ought to bestir ourselves mightily. This is no ordinary time. The times demand something unusual. I want to stand here before you today as one who believes, and believes deeply, seriously, and earnestly, that the whole purpose and objective of this movement today is in the balance. It is for us to turn the scales on the side of right. . . .

"I tell you, my friends, in all seriousness, that today many of our young people are confused and their faith is broken down by what they see and hear. Do you not know this? Is it not the truth? It may be an infallible truth, but many of our young people today do not believe in the Spirit of prophecy because of the inconsistency that they see in the lives of those who ought to be their leaders. If we want the young people to believe, we must set them an example in faith and practice.

"I think the time has come when this setting of a right example should be a challenge to all our people. There is no use of our posing before the world in a certain light, and then shaping our whole course and purpose according to another policy. Oh, may God help us to come back to simplicity and faith, to obedience and right practice. Most of our people know of the standards as taught in the Spirit of Prophecy, and when they see us violating them in our practice, they lose faith, not only in the *Testimonies*, but in our leadership. Let us be consistent leaders. Let us practice what we preach. . . .

"It is not the assaults of our enemies that I fear. No, . . . what I am afraid of is our own departure from the true course. That is the hardest to deal with. . . .

"We are the neediest people on earth. My friends, we need something extraordinary done for us. A great procession is moving toward the kingdom. Are we leading the forces of God in the right direction?

"Threatened By Worldly Conformity

"I believe that the spirit of society, the spirit of the world, has in too many instances come in among us. I would not have you think that I am discouraged over the prospect. No, thank God, I know this movement will move forward triumphantly and victoriously. Nevertheless I feel

I would be remiss if I failed to point out some of the danger signs along the way, and to which I believe we ought to give heed.

"I wish to repeat that many of our parents are distressed over trying to maintain the faith of their sons and daughters because of some things that are taught in some of our classrooms. They come and tell us that some Bible teachers refuse to allow their students to read from 'The Desire of Ages' in a class on the life of Christ. Some come and say the Spirit of prophecy is discredited in the mind and belief of their sons and daughters through interpretations of history that they receive, that those interpretations often are made to discredit the plain statements of the Spirit of prophecy.

"There is another thing that I believe needs attention. It has to do with the social life and the activities in our educational institutions. The faculties need to give more care and attention to some of these matters. I believe that we are developing in some of our educational centers a dress aristocracy that embarrasses the parents of some of the children. Faculties permit the young people to adopt a style of dress that sets the standard for all the students, and if they do not conform, parents and students are embarrassed. It often results in merely a parade of worldly fashion and worldly conformity. I want to lift my voice against it today, and I appeal to you to stop that trend.

* * *

"Too many of our young people are today being led into worldly conformity by some leaders who are themselves adhering to forms of worldly amusement and pleasure. My friends, I wish our young people could be kept away from all the beach parties and nudity parades and moving picture shows and other questionable places where they ought not to go, but where they are sometimes led by their leaders. I believe it is the duty of every school board and every school faculty to take steps to change things. Just how far can we go in this matter of worldly conformity? Let us be done with the spirit of compromise. Let us not be like those people of old who allowed their religious beliefs to be so poisoned by contacts with the world that they were unable to recognize their own Messiah when He appeared.

"Would the pioneers know this movement today if they should awaken? Would they recognize the movement that they started in this world and handed over to their successors? Would they really recognize it? To me, that is a very appealing and important question. 'Oh,' some may say, 'they were a lot of old fogies! They were out of date. They were entirely behind the times. Today, standards have changed.' That is a favorite expression with some, but I do not believe it. I maintain that every right and true and proper standard that has ever prevailed and that is laid down in God's word, is just as vital today as it ever was. I am not one who is willing to admit that standards have changed. That argument suggests that today we have lower standards, and it is used only by those who want lower standards. The nearer we come to the kingdom of God, the higher standards we should have.

* * *

"If Jesus were here today would He recognize us? Indeed, may I say, would we recognize Him? Oh, I trust that the inroads of worldly corruption and poisoning have not prevailed to the place where not even Jesus would recognize us! I feel very solemn and very serious when I think about these things.

* * *

"My friends, really I am concerned about the trends and the tendencies. I confess a great anxiety about them. Here we are today, a group of leaders, and when we leave this place, to what are we going back? We are going back to face thousands of our young people. We are going back to continue to influence and to mold the lives of thousands of young people, and to lead them—but to lead them how? to lead them where?

"A Revival Needed

"What would Jesus say to us today if He were here? Would He undertake to cleanse the temples of our hearts and to drive out the spirit of Sadduceeism, of materialism, of worldly conformity? I believe He would. I believe what we need today, as a group of educators and leaders, more than anything else, is something that cannot come to us from any committee on resolutions, and that is a revival of primitive godliness. Would God that this convention may not close until that something comes to us—not a revival of merely lip service, but a revival of heart and of life, a change of practice, a change that will help us to true up our objectives in this great movement. Today I plead with you all to take your eyes off the world, and fix them upon the Lamb of God which taketh away the sin of the world. Let us talk more about what He is to this movement, than we do about some other things that engage so much of our time and conversation. . . ."—*Review and Herald*, Vol. 114, No. 41, October 14, 1937, pp. 4-6.

O how dreadfully clear it is from every angle viewed that the grisled horses have led the chariot into the world instead of out of it! Even the General Conference President is pleading with these world-loving leaders to amend their ways and their doings (Jer. 7:3). But quitting not their backward course, yet they are retained by the denomination, though they continue leading the people away from God and from the Spirit of Prophecy, and closer to the world and its corrupting influence. And since they are casting out those who are striving to awaken the Laodiceans, will not the General Conference President, in his efforts to awaken, too, arouse to the ironical situation at hand, and instead of longer supporting those self-willed leaders, discharge them, and refellowship the "sighing, crying ones" (*Testimonies*, Vol. 5, p. 210) whom they have cast out?

And while the grisled horses are bringing the tragedy upon themselves by languishing in "the south country," lukewarm and satisfied with their attainments, the bay horses, have "sought to go that they might walk to and fro through the earth"; that is, they have been making ready to go, but could not go until told: "Get you hence, walk to and fro through the earth." Finally, though, they *walk*, signifying that they are honored of God by bearing His standard in triumph to the victory!

In this restraining circumstance, is found proof again of the inerrancy of the *Rod*, for from the beginning, it has proclaimed that the three angels' messages cannot go to the ends of the earth until after the fulfilment of Ezekiel 9, and after the outpouring of the Holy Spirit as described in Joel 2:28—the time in which the Lord has prophetically said, "Go."

Had the present leaders, those who are represented by "the grisled horses," taken heed to the "Call for Reformation," and "had these been little in their own eyes," says the Spirit of Prophecy, and "trusted fully in the Lord, he would have honored them with bearing his standard in triumph to the victory. But they separated from God, yielded to the influence of the world, and the Lord rejected them."—Id., p. 82. "So then because thou art lukewarm, and neither cold nor hot, I *will* spue thee out of My mouth," saith the Lord. Rev. 3:16.

Then will they seek for this "extra oil," but alas too late to profit by any answer to their apprehensive questions: "Are we . . . allowing the mantle to fall from our own shoulders upon the shoulders of others? Are we going to allow others to step into our places and call the world to a reformation. . . ?"

To be sure, "this movement" (chariot) is destined to go forward triumphantly, but only behind the leadership of the bay horses.

The chain of facts linked herein concerning the church's condition is so solidly forged by prophecy and history that none can break it. Indeed each prophetic link is so manifest that even the General Conference President is alarmed. Yet despite this fact, the servant of the Lord predicts that "the light which will lighten the earth with its glory will be called a false light, by those who refuse to walk in its advancing glory."—*Review and Herald*, May 27, 1890.

"In the manifestation of the power that lightens the earth with its glory, they will see only something which in their blindness they think dangerous, something which will arouse their fears and they will brace themselves to resist it. Because the Lord does not work according to their expectations and ideals, they will oppose the work. Why, they say, should we not know the Spirit of God, when we have been in the work so many years?"—*Bible Training School*, 1907, (Reprinted in *Review and Herald*, Nov. 7, 1918).

"We need never expect that when the Lord has light for His people, Satan will stand calmly by, and make no effort to prevent them from receiving it. He will work upon minds to excite distrust and jealousy and unbelief. Let us beware that we do not refuse the light God sends, because it does not come in a way to please us. Let not God's blessing be turned away from us because we know not the time of our visitation. If there are any who do not see and accept the light themselves, let them not stand in the way of others. Let it not be said of this highly favored people, as of the Jews when the good news of the kingdom was preached to them, 'They entered not in themselves, and them that were entering in they hindered.' "—*Testimonies*, Vol. 5, p. 728.

This very sort of thing, we remind our leading brethren, was precisely what occurred in the impious treatment accorded the message of 1888, when it was "slighted, spoken against, ridiculed, . . . rejected," and "denounced as leading to enthusiasm and fanaticism."—*Testimonies to Ministers*, p. 468. Would that that experience never be repeated. Sadly, though, the Spirit of Prophecy says:

"The light which will lighten the earth with its glory will be called a false light. . . . We entreat of you who oppose the light of truth, to stand out of the way of God's people. Let Heaven-sent light shine forth upon them in clear steady rays. God holds you, to whom this light has come, responsible for the use you make of it. Those who will not hear will be held responsible; for the truth has been brought within their reach, but they despised their opportunities and privileges."—*Review and Herald*, May 27, 1890.

That nothing may be left undone to warn them of this terrible disappointment about to overtake them, we address still another appeal

To The Leading Brethren.

Dear Brethren:

Again we plead with you that, even though you despise the source of the plea, you make a thorough investigation of the message that has come to you in the name of the Lord, lest you repeat the history of the Jews. For of all men, you should realize most acutely the dreadful danger of closing your eyes and stopping your ears, even though it be to the words of only some poor "fisherman."

Unless you repent of your present attitude toward the message, "and pray God, if perhaps the thought of thine heart be forgiven thee," then just so surely as your eyes now read these words, your wrong course will bring upon you, and that very shortly, the fulfilment of that fearful pronouncement of the True Witness: "Because thou sayest, I am rich, and increased with goods, and have need of nothing [truth or prophets]," "I will spue thee out of My mouth."

Brethren, remember that "there is no pride so dangerous as spiritual pride."—*Testimonies to Ministers,* p. 109.

Foreseeing that the message was to find you full of self-complacence over your spiritual attainments, the Lord mercifully forewarned you: "Thou art neither cold nor hot"; that is, thou art lukewarm, satisfied. "I would thou wert cold or hot",—dissatisfied,—wanting everything rather than feeling that you have need of nothing. Then you would not by your actions be saying, "I am rich, and increased with goods, and have need of nothing,"—neither truth nor prophets,—but would know that "thou art wretched, and miserable, and poor, and blind, and naked."

Brethren, may these disillusioning words open your eyes that you may see yourselves as you are, so that "the shame of thy nakedness do not appear." The promise is unfailing: "Anoint thine eyes with eye-salve, that thou mayest see." Our prayers are that you fail not, for we love you.

Remember that though the Lord in His great mercy has called you out of darkness to walk in His marvelous light, yet if you walk not therein, your light shall become darkness and your goods a booty.

Says the Lord: "I have caused thee to multiply as the bud of the field, and thou hast increased and waxen great, and thou art come to excellent ornaments: thy breasts are fashioned, and thine hair is grown, whereas thou wast naked and bare." Ezek. 16:7. But "as many as I love, I rebuke and chasten: be zealous therefore, and repent." Rev. 3:19. Or "therefore will I return, and take away My corn in the time thereof, and My wine in the season thereof, and will recover My wool and My flax given to cover her nakedness." Hos. 2:9.

Take heed, Brethren, lest by your wilful course you incur God's displeasure and (speaking in the mixed figures of these correlative prophecies) in His awful wrath He strip you naked, and "spue thee out of

[His] mouth." Then you will be "hot," but to no avail, for it will be forever too late to change, and though like Esau you shall weep bitterly the Lord shall not hear you.

No more honest in their deception than are you in yours, yet the Jews at least gave audience to Christ, whereas you have not been that fair. Notwithstanding that Inspiration characterizes you as "blind" and in "a terrible deception" (*Testimonies*, Vol. 3, p. 254), you are setting yourselves up as wise spiritual guides, even demanding that Inspiration bow down to your decision as to what shall or what shall not be brought before God's people! Your behavior is as unreasonable as the strictures of the ancient scribes and Pharisees against the teachings of Christ!

Increasingly your challenging attitude toward the present revelations from God's Word, is crying out: "Who is the Lord, that I should obey His voice to *let Israel go?* I know not the Lord neither will I let Israel go." Ex. 5:2.

The Lord's counsel is: "Precious light is to shine forth from the Word of God, and let no one presume to dictate what shall or what shall not be brought before the people in the messages of enlightenment that He shall send, and so quench the Spirit of God. *Whatever* may be his position of *authority*, *no one* has a right to shut away the light from the people."—*Testimonies on Sabbath School Work*, p. 65.

"God means what He says."—*Testimonies,* Vol. 5, p. 365.

"Men . . . through selfishness . . . crowd down the very ones whom God is using to diffuse the light He has given them . . . Satan's skill is exercised. . . . He works to *restrict religious liberty.* . . . Organizations . . . will work under Satan's dictation to bring men under the control of men; and fraud and guile will bear the semblance of zeal for truth and for the advancement of the kingdom of God. . . . such men assume to exercise the prerogatives of God,—they presume to do that which God Himself will not do in seeking to control the minds of men. Thus they follow in the track of Romanism. . . . In such arrangements *the man who allows his mind to be ruled* by the mind of another is thus separated from God and exposed to temptation. . . . but God has plainly set it before us. He says, 'Cursed be the man that trusteth in man, and maketh flesh his arm.'"—*Testimonies,*Vol. 7, pp. 179, 180, 181, 178.

Calling yourselves men of "experience," you say: "If a brother has any light on the Scriptures, let him submit it to us, and if we see no light in it, let him drop it." But, Brethren, how can you see light in anything without looking into it? And how can you discern spiritual things unless you "anoint thine eyes with eyesalve ["revealed truth"], that thou mayest see"? Refusing to do this, how will you ever discern truth?

Why should we renounce the message in the *Rod* when you have so utterly failed to prove it to be in error? Why cast aside precious gems of truth simply because the majority cannot tell them from paste jewels? You have long been leveling stout words against the tyrannies of others, but now how about your own! You charge that our position "puts us in bad company." But you do not realize what you say, and that we stand in identically the same position today as did John the Baptist, Christ, the apostles, Luther, and Miller in the yesterdays, and as did the founders of the S. D. A. denomination; not in the position which you are trying to make us appear to be in—that which the opposers of truth have always occupied, and by which thousands have been cheated of heaven's blessing! Brethren, really prove us wrong, and you will *then* see how quickly we will change our position!

Our unfailing concern is that you will take heed to the counsel of the True Witness, and confess your poverty of spiritual things, lest He pronounce upon you the dreadful woe: "Howl, ye shepherds, and cry; and wallow yourselves in the ashes, ye *principal* of the flock: for the days of your *slaughter* and of your dispersions are accomplished; and ye shall fall like a pleasant vessel" (Jer. 25:34), and thus be missing when "it shall come to pass afterward, that I will pour out My Spirit upon all flesh; and your sons and your daughters shall prophesy, your old men shall dream dreams, your young men shall see visions: and also upon the servants and upon the handmaids in those days will I pour out My Spirit." Joel 2:28, 29. Speaking of this time, the Spirit of Prophecy declares: "Mighty miracles were wrought, the sick were healed, and signs and wonders followed the believers."—*Early Writings*, p. 278.

O what unbounding folly and loss to pursue a wrong course, and lose out in a time like this, when the privilege is being accorded you to choose rather to "sit down with Abraham, and Isaac, and Jacob, in the kingdom of heaven"! Matt. 8:11. May you not fail.

Sincerely yours for a humble spirit and the happy choice,

Your friend and servant.

Though exceedingly burdened for our leading brethren that they lay to heart the Lord's counsel just tendered, we are likewise burdened that the laity also lay well to heart the Lord's counsel to them. Thus, impartially, we now address

A Word to The Elect of God, The 144,000!

Dear Brethren:

To you who hear the voice of the Good Shepherd, and who are not known to us by name, but only by prospective number

(144,000) and office (God's guileless servants, kings and priests),—to each of you comes the solemn certainty that the sealing time is very short, its end very near. Therefore, Brother, Sister, make sure that you receive the seal of God on time; do not delay the return to our Eden home. "Today if ye will hear His voice, harden not your hearts." Heb. 4:7. He that is on the Lord's side, let him tarry no longer. The time has fully arrived for the 144,000 to come into line with God's program for the finishing of His work and the preparing of them for translation. So, saith the Lord: "As a shepherd seeketh out his flock in the day that he is among his sheep that are scattered; so will I seek out My sheep, and will deliver them out of all places where they have been scattered in the cloudy and dark day." Ezek. 34:12. "And the Lord their God shall save them in that day as the flock of His people: for they shall be as the stones of a crown, lifted up as an *ensign* upon His land." Zech. 9:16.

Make haste Brother, Sister; immediately take your stand on the Lord's side, so that He may, because of your "sighing" (repenting) and "crying" (proclaiming the sealing message), without delay disclose "to view" as the "servants of our God," you who shall escape being among the "slain of the Lord," be sent unto the Gentiles, and "bring *all* your *brethren* . . . out of *all nations*." Isa. 66:16, 19, 20.

Study the message for yourselves, and forbid that any flesh interfere with your salvation. Make your own decision independently of any man, and know for yourself that God is leading you as He did when you were to become as S. D. A. Accept neither priest nor prelate as your God. "Be ye not as the horse, or as the mule, which have no understanding: whose mouth must be held in with bit and bridle, lest they come near unto thee." Ps. 32:9. Why should you trip and fall over the same stumbling block which has plunged millions headlong into hell? Look up, Brother, Sister, and avoid the calamity ahead, and help others also to avoid it.

And as for those who are deaf to the voice of the Good Shepherd, "my soul shall weep in secret places for your pride; and mine eye shall weep sore and run down with tears, because the Lord's flock is carried away captive." Jer. 13:17." Therefore hear the counsel of the Lord, that He hath taken against Edom; and His purposes, that He hath purposed against the inhabitants." Jer. 49:20. "And the shepherds shall have no way to flee, nor the principal of the flock to escape." Jer. 25:35.

Now our great desire and hope is that each one of you will communicate with us without delay, so that in accordance with God's Word we may together launch a program for the "siege," and in such a manner that we can present to the enemy a united front. Then will God work; then will the barriers which have been erected against the Truth and against His servants who are to "be disclosed to view," fall like the walls of Jericho! "He that hath an ear, let him hear what the Spirit saith unto the churches." Rev. 3:22.

Yours is "to bind up the brokenhearted, to proclaim liberty to the captives, and the opening of the prison to them that are bound; to proclaim the acceptable year of the Lord, and the day of vengeance of our God; to comfort all that mourn." Isa. 61:1, 2. What an unmatched privilege! God forbid that any forfeit it.

> Sincerely yours for implicit trust in God and for green pasture for His flock,

> Your friend and servant.

P. S. Avail yourselves of the publications containing Present Truth, and get ready for the work. Be of the "wise," and fill your "vessels" with this extra "oil" for your "lamps." Our literature will fully reveal that "the days are at hand, and the effect of every vision." Ezek. 12:23. That is to say, the visions of the prophets, which appeared to be full of mysteries, are now become plain facts.

Twelve tracts, to date, aggregating 898 pages, will be sent free of charge and postpaid to anyone, upon request. To those newly requesting the literature, the series will be forwarded one number at a time at two-week intervals. Those who accompany their requests with names of S. D. A.'s, may, if they so specify, have all the twelve tracts together.

"*Receive My instruction, and not silver; and knowledge rather than choice gold.*"—Prov. 8:10. "Today if ye will hear His voice harden not your hearts." Order now.

Address all orders to The Universal Publishing Association, P.O. Box 24027, Waco, Texas 76702, U. S. A. or visit us on the web at UniversalPublishing.com.

SCRIPTURAL INDEX